COOKING WITH CHEF JEAN

A practical cooking guide for young students learning how to cook.

VOLUME 1

Introduction

Chef Jean is a French chef graduated from ISTHIA (Université Toulouse – Jean Jaures) and have years of experience in teaching culinary to students varying from primary school age to higher education in forms of physical and online classes.

Other than teaching, Chef Jean provides his expertise in private dining and catering under his company Dalí by chef Jean in Kuala Lumpur (Malaysia).

Beside his activity which is his passion, Chef Jean is involved in Rugby association in Malaysia and spend his time between Reunion Island and Toulouse to find culinary inspirations and enjoy his family.

About this book

This book follows a user-friendly sequence whereby recipes are shared, along with a short history and fun facts about the origins and cultural importance of each dish. Then, ingredients are listed, followed by a step-by-step guide on how to cook each recipe, as well as top tips from the grand master Chef Jean as well!

The recipes are specially designed by the chef to be made by the kids with clear instructions. They are all been tested and approved during our cooking class in the best international schools in Kuala Lumpur.

This book can accompany an after school cooking course, such as the one offered by Chef Jean and his colleagues, or used by parents wishing to teach classic, simple recipes to their children.

Dedication

**For Antoine and Pablo, in memory
of the good times spent in the kitchen**
- Chef Jean

For Ariella and Leonard
- Dylan

Acknowledgements

A big thanks to our friends and family for the ongoing support and good humour while we made this book.

A special mention, as always, to the fabulous Cooking Community of GIS, LFKL, ISKL, BSKL and Alice Smith for their support and feedback throughout the creation process of this book.

Thank you to Karine and Dylan for their time spent reading, re-reading, proofreading and editing this book.

Lastly, thank you to all the schools and parents for trusting us to teach their kids cooking and baking. We really have a blast doing it!

Follow chef Jean on :

 **www.chefjeankl.com**

 **@chefjeankl**
@dalíbychefjean (private dining in Malaysia and South East Asia)
@cuisineboleh (kids, adults, corporate cooking classes)

 **@chefjeankl**
@dalíbychefjean
@cuisineboleh

TABLE OF CONTENTS

	RECIPES	Page
INTRO	The Tools of the Trade	1
1	Chocolate Eclair	4
2	Spider Pasta Carbonara	9
3	Smarties Cookie	13
4	Chicken Lasagna	17
5	Lava Cake	21
6	Halloween Cupcake	24
7	Pizza	28
8	Vanilla Mille Feuille	32
9	Sausage Croissant	36
10	Mushroom Quiche	40
11	Pavlova	44
12	Gingerbread Man	48

Baking Tray:
A baking tray, also known as a baking sheet or cookie sheet, is a flat metal tray with raised edges. It's essential for baking cookies, roasting vegetables, and making sheet cakes.

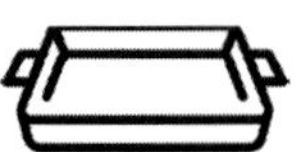

Brush: A brush, such as a pastry brush or basting brush, is handy for applying butter, oil, or glazes to pastries, bread, or roasts. It helps to distribute liquids evenly and adds flavor and shine to your creations.

Cling Film: Cling film, also known as plastic wrap or cling wrap, is a transparent plastic film used to cover bowls, plates, or wrap food to keep it fresh. It helps seal in flavors and protects ingredients from drying out or absorbing unwanted odors.

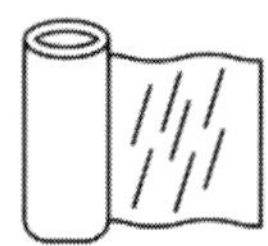

Cookie Cutters:
Cookie cutters come in various shapes and sizes and are perfect for making fun-shaped cookies, sandwiches, or even cutting out fruit shapes.

Measuring Cups and Spoons:
Measuring cups and spoons help us learn about different measurements and practice accuracy when adding ingredients to recipes.

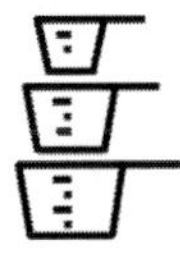

Mixing Bowls:
We use mixing bowls to combine ingredients, mix batters, and toss salads. Opt for bowls that are lightweight and non-slip to make it easier for them to handle.

Parchment Paper:
Parchment paper is a non-stick paper that can be placed on baking trays to prevent food from sticking. It's also useful for creating a clean work surface when rolling out dough or for wrapping foods for baking or steaming.

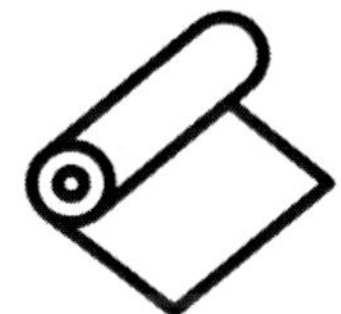

Pastry Bag/Piping Bag:
Essential for the art of piping! We use these to pipe whipped cream, frosting, or even decorate cakes and cookies with precision.

Ramekins:
Ramekins are small ceramic or glass dishes that are useful for individual servings of desserts like crème brûlée or custards. They can also be used for portioning ingredients or holding small dipping sauces.

Rolling Pin:
A rolling pin is great for rolling out dough for cookies, pizza, or pie crusts.

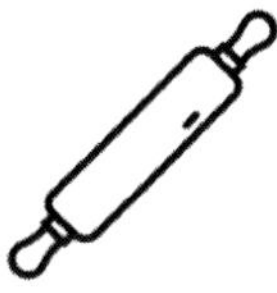

Saucepan:
A saucepan is a versatile cooking vessel with high sides and a handle that is used for various purposes in the kitchen. It's ideal for heating and simmering sauces, boiling water for pasta & cooking soups

Spatula:
Use this tool to scrape bowls clean, mix ingredients, and flip pancakes or omelets without scratching non-stick pans.

Weighing scale:
A weighing scale, also known as a kitchen scale, is an essential tool for precise measurements in baking. It helps us accurately weigh ingredients like flour, sugar, and butter. This ensures that our recipes turn out just right and helps us understand the importance of precise measurements in baking.

Whisk:
We use it to beat eggs, whisk together dry ingredients, and mix dressings or sauces.

Wooden Spoon:
A wooden spoon is a versatile tool used for stirring, mixing, and blending ingredients while cooking or baking. It's gentle on pots and pans and doesn't conduct heat like metal, making it safe to use in hot liquids or on non-stick surfaces.

RECIPE 1:
Chocolate Éclair

FRENCH NAME: *Éclair au chocolat*

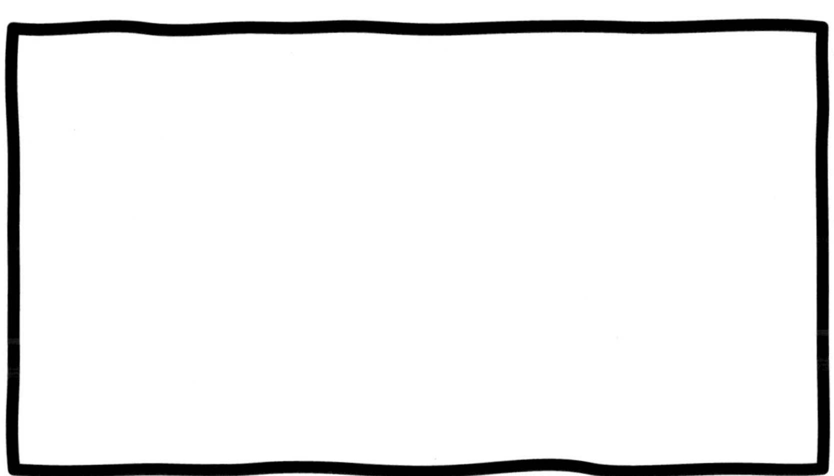

HISTORY

At the origin, *"l'éclair"* was called Duchess Bread *"pain à la duchesse"* which was a finger shaped choux pastry rolled in almonds.
In the XIX century, Antonin Carème, one of the great, if not perhaps the very greatest, pastry chefs of all time had the idea to take out the almonds, fill it with chocolate pastry cream and cover it with melted sugar. "L'éclair" was born.

COOKING NOTES

Master this easy recipe and you can make many pastries most bakers are scared to try: Pipe choux with whipped cream for **cream puff** or ice cream for **profiteroles**, mix it with cheese and herbs for savory **gougères** or deep fry it for **churros**!

INGREDIENTS

Choux Pastry

- Water — 250g
- Butter — 60g
- Sugar — 10g
- Salt — 5g
- Flour — 150g
- Eggs — 3 (grade A)

Chocolate Custard

- Milk — 300ml
- Eggs — 4
- Sugar — 50g
- Cornstarch — 30g
- Chocolate — 100g

Chocolate icing

- White fondant — 250g
- Cacao powder — 1 tablespoon
- Water — 1 tablespoon

METHOD

Preparation: Éclair

- Combine water, butter, sugar and salt in a pot and bring to the boil.
- Add all the flour at once.
- Stir on the heat with wooden spoon until it forms into a dough.
- Dry out for several seconds until it no longer sticks to the pan nor the wooden spoon.
- Transfer dough into a bowl and let it cool for a few minutes.
- Add in eggs one by one.
- Line the baking tray with parchment paper.
- Pipe the éclair pastry.
- Bake for 10 minutes at 200°C, then 15 minutes at 180°C.

Preparation: Chocolate Custard

- Warm the milk in the saucepan until you start to see wisps of steam. It should not actually be boiling.
- Make the egg-sugar base: In a medium bowl, whisk together the sugar, flour, and salt. Add the egg yolks and whisk them into the dry ingredients. This will form a thick paste.
- Add the milk to the egg mixture: Pour a little of the hot milk into the eggs and whisk to combine. Continue pouring all the milk slowly into the eggs, whisking continuously.
- Pour everything back into the saucepan.
- Whisk constantly. At first, the pastry cream will look very thin and frothy, but it will start to thicken after a few minutes. When it has thickened to a pudding-like consistency, pause whisking every few seconds to see if the cream has come to a boil. If you see large bubbles popping on the surface, whisk for a few more seconds and then remove the pan from heat.
- With a double boiler, melt the chocolate and add it to the custard. Plastic wrap and place in the fridge.

Preparation: Chocolate icing

- Mix egg white with icing sugar and cacao powder.

Preparation: Final step

- Fill shells with chocolate custard and re-cover the top with the chocolate icing.

REFLECTION

With this recipe I learned:

____

____

____

When I make this again, one thing I might do differently is:

____

____

____

The end product tasted really:

____

____

____

CHEF JEAN'S TOP TIPS

RECIPE 2:

Spider Pasta "Carbo" sauce

FRENCH NAME: *Pâtes 'Carbo' en araignées*

BACKGROUND INFO

During World War II, in 1944, an American soldier prepared some spaghetti, but it was so poor that he mixed his ration K, the preparation for all soldiers, into the pasta. It was made up of powdered eggs, bacon and liquid cream. The result was perfect. Carbonara was born like this, almost by accident!

COOKING NOTES

Preparing a carbonara dish allows you to develop essential cooking techniques. Key skills are how to cook perfectly pasta to achieve an *al dente* texture, and how to create a creamy sauce.

Real Carbonara does not have cream in the sauce. The creaminess of the sauce comes from the combination of raw eggs and cheese. For safety reasons, we will use cream in our recipe and no raw eggs.

INGREDIENTS

Spider Pasta "Carbo" sauce

-	Spaghetti	250g
-	Chicken sausage	200g
-	Liquid cream	75ml
-	Chopped onions	1
-	Olive oil	1 tablespoon
-	Garlic	1 clove
-	Salt	1 teaspoon
-	Parmesan	100g

METHOD

Spider Pasta

- Put a large saucepan of water to boil.

- Add 1 teaspoon of salt to the boiling water.

- Cut the sausage into 6 small bites.

- Insert spaghetti inside bites.

- Cook it for about 8 minutes or until *al dente* (just cooked).

Creamy "Carbo" sauce

- Finely grate 100g parmesan cheese.
- Gently squash 2 peeled plump garlic cloves with the blade of a knife, just to bruise it.
- In a pan with olive oil, stir onions, garlic, salt, pepper.
- Add cream, let it reduce for a few minutes.
- When the pasta is ready, lift it from the water with a pasta fork or tongs and put it in the frying pan.
- Add parmesan.
- Add chopped basil.

Assembling

Combine the spider pasta and the sauce together.
Serve on a plate and decorate with parmesan and basil leaves.

REFLECTION

With this recipe I learned:

____

____

____

When I make this again, one thing I might do differently is:

____

____

____

The end product tasted really:

____

____

____

CHEF JEAN'S TOP TIPS

RECIPE 3:

Smarties Cookies

FRENCH NAME: Cookies aux Smarties

HISTORY

Cookies appear to have their origins in 7th century AD Persia, shortly after the use of sugar became relatively common in the region. They spread to Europe through the Muslim conquest of Spain. By the 14th century, they were common in all levels of society throughout Europe, from royal cuisine to street vendors.

COOKING NOTES

Preparing home made cookies offers an opportunity to develop fundamental baking skills. Key skills include accurately measuring ingredients and creaming butter and sugar to achieve a light and fluffy texture. You will also learn to adjust temperature and baking time in order to get optimal results!

INGREDIENTS

Smarties cookies

-	Sugar	180g
-	Soft Butter	200g
-	Vanilla extract	1 teaspoon
-	Flour	350g
-	Eggs	2
-	Baking powder	1 teaspoon
-	Smarties	150g

METHOD

Preparation: Smarties cookies

- Pre heat your oven, fan bake at 180°.
- Measure the ingredients.
- Combine the dry ingredients: flour, sugar, salt, baking powder together.
- Cream together butter, sugar and vanilla.
- Add eggs one by one.
- Beat the mixture.
- Add dry ingredients and stir until just combined.

- Add the smarties and beat until they are evenly distributed and the cookie dough is easy to roll. It should not not be dry or crumbly.
- Once the cookie dough is finished, it's time to portion and roll the dough. This can be done in 2 ways:
    1) Using a ice cream scoop.
    2) Using hands to make small balls.
- Place on baking tray, leaving some space between them.
- Stick a few more smarties on top.
- Cook cookies 180°/ 10mn.

REFLECTION

With this recipe I learned:

____

____

____

When I make this again, one thing I might do differently is:

____

____

____

The end product tasted really:

____

____

____

RECIPE 4:

Chicken Lasagne

FRENCH NAME: Lasagnes au poulet

HISTORY:

Most reports seem to indicate that this pasta dish (as we know it) made its first appearance in the Italian city of Naples during the Middle Ages. However, while many of us associate lasagna pasta with Italy, there are others who also believe that lasagna originated in Greece or England.

COOKING NOTES:

Preparing Chicken Lasagna can teach you many key skills such as how to make a **roux** (French mother sauce), how to make a **tomato sauce** amd how to **layer ingredients**. The choice of filling can vary according to your taste. Popular alternatives are salmon and different vegetables.

INGREDIENTS

Ingredients: Main dish

-	Lasagna pasta	250g
-	Minced chicken	150g
-	Chopped onions	20g
-	Crushed garlic	2 cloves
-	Tomato sauce	200g
-	Cheese (mozzarella, cheddar)	100g
-	Salt & pepper to taste	

Ingredients: Béchamel

-	Milk	250g
-	Corn starch	25g
-	Nutmeg powder	to taste
-	Salt & pepper	to taste

METHOD

Preparation:

1. **Preheat oven to 175°C**

2. **Prepare the Garnish**
- Stir 10g onions, garlic and add minced chicken, salt & pepper.

- After 5 minutes, add spinach, salt & pepper.

- Add tomato sauce to the chicken.

3. **Prepare the béchamel**
- Mix corn starch and cold milk.

- Stir on the stove and continue to whisk until it's thick.

4. **Layer up the lasagna**
- In a baking dish place one layer of pasta.

- Pour on a layer of béchamel.

- Pour chicken and spinach tomato sauce.

- Top with another layer of lasagna.

- Repeat the process until you reach the top of the baking dish.

- Finish with one layer of béchamel and sprinkle with cheese.

- Bake until top is brown and lasagna pasta is cooked.

With this recipe I learned:

____

____

____

When I make this again, one thing I might do differently is:

____

____

____

The end product tasted really:

____

____

____

CHEF JEAN'S TOP TIPS

Bonjour!
How to check the doneness of your lasagna? Lasagna is done when it reaches an internal temperature of at least 165 degrees Celsius. You can also check for doneness by inserting a toothpick or fork into the center of your lasagne. If it comes away clean, it's ready to eat.

RECIPE 5:

Lava Cake

FRENCH NAME: Fondant au chocolat

HISTORY
The legendary French chef Michel Bras likes to think he invented the chocolate fondant in 1981: patenting his recipe for individual cakes, baked with frozen ganache inside that, when cooked, turned into a runny centre.

COOKING NOTES
Preparing lava cake can teach you many key skills such as how to **melt chocolate** (microwave or 'bain marie') and also how to bake perfectly in the oven to keep the lava texture in the middle of the cake.

INGREDIENTS

Lava cake

-	Dark chocolate 60/70%	250g
-	Butter	200g
-	Sugar	200g
-	Flour	70g
-	Eggs	4

METHOD

- Preheat oven to 180°C. Generously butter 5 (4 oz) ramekins; set aside.
- In a medium microwave-safe bowl, melt chocolate and butter in 30-second increments.
- In a separate large bowl, whisk the eggs and sugar until pale and fluffy.
- Whisk in the melted chocolate along with the flour.
- Divide batter into ramekins and place them on a baking sheet.
- Bake for 5 minutes or until the edges begin to pull away from the ramekins but the center is still jiggly.
- Remove from oven and serve immediately with ice cream.

REFLECTION

With this recipe I learned:

When I make this again, one thing I might do differently is:

The end product tasted really:

CHEF JEAN'S TOP TIPS

RECIPE 6:

Halloween Cupcake

FRENCH NAME: Cupcake d'Halloween

BACKGROUND INFO
Halloween is a holiday celebrated each year on October 31. The tradition originated with the ancient Celtic festival of Samhain, when people would light bonfires and wear costumes to ward off ghosts. In the eighth century, Pope Gregory III designated November 1st as a time to honor all saints. Soon, All Saints Day incorporated some of the traditions of Samhain. The evening before was known as All Hallows Eve, and later Halloween. Over time, Halloween evolved into a day of activities like trick-or-treating, carving jack-o-lanterns, festive gatherings, donning costumes and eating treats.

COOKING NOTES
Preparing Halloween cupcakes can teach you many key skills such as how to make a batter, how to use food coloring, how to make frosting and how to use pipping bags for decoration.

INGREDIENTS

Cupcake (10 pieces)

-	Flour	140g
-	Melted butter	120g
-	Sugar	100g
-	Eggs	2
-	Milk	3 tablespoons
-	Baking	6g
-	Vanilla extract	1 teaspoons
-	Lemon zest	5g

Deco mummies

-	White fondant	100g
-	Rasberry jam	50g
-	Red or orange Smarties	20
-	Black edible pen	

METHOD

Cupcake

- Preheat oven to 180°C.
- Mix the butter and sugar with a whisk until you achieve a pale colour and fluffy texture.
- Add eggs, one at a time, scraping down the sides of the bowl after each addition.
- Stir in the flour and baking powder to the mixture and stir with a spatula.
- Dissolve all with milk.
- Add vanilla and combine all the ingredients.
- Divide the mixture in a muffin covered with baking cups and bake for 13 min, 180°C.
- Remove from the oven and let cool.

Fondant icing

- Dust your work station with icing sugar
- Spread the sugar paste 2-3mm thick using a rolling pin
- Cut strips approximately 5 mm wide

Decoration

- Spread raspberry jam on the top of your muffin.
- Decorate your cupcakes with the strips of dough in sugar and add smarties for the eyes and then paint (with edible pen) for pupils.

REFLECTION

With this recipe I learned:

When I make this again, one thing I might do differently is:

The end product tasted really:

CHEF JEAN'S TOP TIPS

RECIPE 7:

Pizza Margherita

FRENCH NAME: Pizza Margherita (c'est pareil!)

BACKGROUND INFO

According to the popular legend, the pizza Margherita was invented in 1899 by Raffaele Esposito, chef at Pizzeria Brandi. The pizza was allegedly created in honor of Italy's unification, with the three toppings (basil, mozzarella and tomato) respectively representing the Green, White and red of the italian flag.

COOKING NOTES

Preparing pizza margherita can teach you many key skills such as how to make a pizza douch which is very similar from bread dough, how to use yeast and how to roll the pizza dough using a rolling pin

INGREDIENTS

Pizza dough

-	Flour	250g
-	Salt	5g
-	Yeast	5g
-	Water	125g
-	Olive oil	25g

Garnish

-	Tomato sauce	20g
-	Shredded mozzarella	50g
-	Cherry tomato	3 (sliced)
-	Basil	a few leaves

METHOD

Pizza Dough

- In a medium bowl, mix flour, salt and yeast together.
- Pour in warm water and the olive oil and bring together with a wooden spoon until you have a soft, fairly wet dough.
- Knead the dough for about 15 minutes, until smooth.
- Make a ball with dough, place it in the bowl.
- Cover with a tea towel and set aside for 1 hour or until it doubles in size.
- Before shaping the dough, heat the oven to 220°C.
- When the dough is ready, punch it down to remove the gas and roll it into a circle shape.

Assembling

- Add the tomato sauce using a table spoon and spread it out with the back of the spoon.
- Add the shredded mozzarella.
- Bake for 10 minutes at 220°C.
- Decorate with basil leaves and drizzle virgin olive oil.
- Serve hot.

REFLECTION

With this recipe I learned:

____

____

____

When I make this again, one thing I might do differently is:

____

____

____

The end product tasted really:

____

____

____

CHEF JEAN'S TOP TIPS

RECIPE 8:
Vanilla Mille-Feuilles

FRENCH NAME: Mille-feuilles à la vanille

BACKGROUND INFO

Despite its widespread popularity, we know very little about the mille-feuille's background, and its exact origins are unknown. Mention of the mille-feuille dates back to 1600s France, when gastronomic chronicler Francois Piere de la Varenne recorded it in an early cook book. However, a century later, renowned chef to the aristocracy and Pioneer of french haute cuisine Antonin Carême enigmatically referred to it as an ancient recipe. At the time, the dessert was more poetically named *gâteau de mille feuilles* or "cake of a thousand leaves".

COOKING NOTES

Preparing vanilla mille-feuilles can teach you many key skills such as how to make a pastry cream, how to caramelize the puff pastry and keep it flat, how to use a piping bag and finally, how to use a sieve for the decoration.

INGREDIENTS

Puff pastry

- Puff pastry (already rolled)   500g

Vanilla Custard

- White fine Sugar   40g
- Milk   250g
- Flour   35g
- Egg yolks   3
- Vanila extract   1 teaspoon

Decoration

- Icing sugar   100g

METHOD

Vanilla Custard

- Bring the milk with vanilla to boil, then remove from the heat and set aside.
- Mix together egg yolk and sugar until pale colour and smooth texture.
- Add flour and whisk.
- Temper the mixture by drizzling in about 1/4 cup of the hot milk while whisking. Whisk in the remaining milk then pour back into your pot and place over medium heat.
- Whisk on the stove until custard become thick.
- Transfer the vanila custard in a bowl, cover with plastic wrap and reserve in the fridge.

Puff Pastry

- Pre heat oven to190°C.
- Cut the puff pastry dough into triangles (2X4 inch per individual pastry).
- Transfer the rectangles onto a parchment-lined baking sheet then cover with another sheet of paper and a heavy baking tray or a baking sheet. You can weigh the top down with pastry weights if it's a super-light tray, we don't want the pastry to puff up too much in the oven.
- Bake for about 10 to 12 minutes, till the dough is a nice golden brown and crispy texture.

Assembling

- Transfer the pastry cream to a piping bag fitted with a larger round tip and pipe dollops onto one of the pastry pieces.
- Place a second pastry piece on top and sprinkle icing sugar with a small strainer.

REFLECTION

With this recipe I learned:

____

____

____

When I make this again, one thing I might do differently is:

____

____

____

The end product tasted really:

____

____

____

**CHEF JEAN'S
TOP TIPS**

35

RECIPE 9:

Sausage Croissant

FRENCH NAME: Croissant saucisse béchamel

BACKGROUND INFO

I have two or three recipes I use to take care of any tired or slightly dried out croissants and this one is one of my favorite. The béchamel sauce is easy, fast and very tasty. Moreover, you will now be able to reycle your old croissants into something really delicious.

COOKING NOTES

Preparing chicken sausage croissants can teach you many key skills such as how to recycle a croissant which is already 1 or 2 days old into a delicious food. This recipe will also give you another chance to master the technique of making a top quality béchamel sauce.

INGREDIENTS

Sausage croissants: 4 pieces

- Croissants 4
- Chicken sausage 1 per croissant

Béchamel Sauce

- Milk 250g
- Flour 30g
- Butter 30g
- Salt to taste
- Pepper to taste
- Grated cheese 100g

METHOD

Béchamel saucel:

- Melt the butter in a heavy-bottomed saucepan. Stir in the flour and cook, stirring constantly, until the paste cooks and bubbles a bit, but don't let it brown.
- After 1 minute, Add the milk, continuing to stir as the sauce thickens.
- Bring it to a boil.
- Add salt and pepper to taste, lower the heat, and cook, stirring for 2 to 3 minutes more.
- Remove from the heat.

Assembling :

- Preheat oven to 200°C.
- Cut the croissant on the top (don't fully cut it).
- Spread the inside with béchamel.
- Add the chicken sausage inside. Top with remaining béchamel sauce, then top with remaining cheese.
- Bake until cheese is brown and bubbling. Usually it takes 8 minutes at 190°C.

REFLECTION

With this recipe I learned:

____

____

____

When I make this again, one thing I might do differently is:

____

____

____

The end product tasted really:

____

____

____

CHEF JEAN'S TOP TIPS

Bonjour! Ça va? If your béchamel sauce is too thick, add a bit of milk until it reaches the consistency that you like. The sauce should be slightly thick, but you want it just liquid enough to pour.

RECIPE 10:

Mushroom Quiche

FRENCH NAME: *Quiche aux champignons*

BACKGROUND INFO

The Word 'quiche' comes from the Lorraine – Franconian (a German dialect spoken in the region of Lorraine in France) word "küeche", meaning "cake". Although now considered to be a founding dish of French cuisine, the quiche originated in German and pastry tarts with custard and meat, fish or fruit fillings can be traced back to 14th century England.

COOKING NOTES

Preparing a mushroom quiche offers an opportunity to develop various culinary skills. Key skills include mastering pastry-making. You will learn to sauté mushrooms to perfection and understand the art of blending ingredients to achieve a balanced flavour profile.

INGREDIENTS

Short bread crust

-	Flour	200g
-	Soft Butter	100g
-	Salt	½ teaspoon
-	Water	1 tablespoon
-	Egg	1

Savoury Custard

-	Milk	50g
-	Cream	200g
-	Egg	2
-	Salt	½ teaspoon
-	Pepper	½ teaspoon

Garnish

-	Mushroom	400g
-	Olive oil	1 tablespoon
-	Grated Cheese	100g

METHOD

Short bread crust

- Mix together flour, butter and salt with fingers.
- Add egg and water, then mix it with fingers.
- Form a ball and put it in fridge for 30 minutes.
- Pre heat oven at 180°C.
- Roll the pastry out on a floured work surface or roll it into 2 pieces parchment paper then fit it in a tart mould.
- Do dots with fork and blind bake it 10 minutes until it's light brown.

Savoury Custard

- In a bowl, mix all the ingredients together (milk, cream, egg, salt & pepper).

Garnish & Assembling

- In a pan, heat olive oil and cook mushroom with salt and pepper.
- Once the short bread crust is light brown, fill with the garnish, and the savoury custard.
- Top with cheese.
- Bake it for 20 to 30 minutes at 180°C.

REFLECTION

With this recipe I learned:

When I make this again, one thing I might do differently is:

The end product tasted really:

CHEF JEAN'S TOP TIPS

Bonjour! Ça va? You can add a dash of crushed garlic and chopped parsley inside the mushroom, it's going to add color and taste to the garnish.
You can keep some in the freezer and take them out when needed. They handle the cold very well. Don't forget to protect them with clingwrap to avoid them getting "freezer' taste.

RECIPE 11:

Pavlova

FRENCH NAME: *Pavlova*

BACKGROUND INFO

Pavlova is a meringue based dessert. This dessert is believed to have been created in honour of the russian ballerina Anna Pavlova either during or after one of her tours to Australia and New Zealand in the 1920s.

Taking the form of a cake-like circular block of baked meringue, pavlova has a crisp crust and soft, light inside. The confection is usually topped with fruit and whipped cream.

COOKING NOTES

Preparing pavlova can teach you many key skills such as how to make meringue, how to use an electric mixer and how to prepare a delicious Chantilly cream.

INGREDIENTS

Meringue:

- Egg whites   4
- Sugar   190g
- Vanilla extract   2 drops
- Corn starch   1 tablespoon

Chantilly cream:

- Cream   250g
- Sugar   2 tablespoon

Fruits:

- Strawberries   1 box (200g)
- Peaches in syrup   1 can
- Dragon fruit   1 piece

METHOD

Meringue:

- Pre heat oven at 100°C.

- Whisk the egg whites at a high speed with an electric whisk. When they become foamy, gradually add the sugar.

- Add a few drops of vanilla essence and 1tablespoon of corn starch. Whisk until you get stiff peaks.

- Pipe a nest shape with a nice star nozzle and cook for 1h15 at 100°C.

Chantilly cream:

- Whip the cream and sugar until it becomes thick.

Fruits:

- Cut the fruits lengthwise to add volume.

- Fill the meringue with Chantilly cream and then decorate with the fruit. This is your chance to make the pavlova really beautiful!

- Keep the pavlova in the fridge.

REFLECTION

With this recipe I learned:

____

____

____

When I make this again, one thing I might do differently is:

____

____

____

The end product tasted really:

____

____

____

CHEF JEAN'S TOP TIPS

Bonjour! Ça va? Feel free to play around with fruits. In this recipe, we choose fruits you can easily find in Malaysia. Cherry on the cake, do not hesitate to do your own red fruit coulis (made with frozen raspberry/strawberries coulis + sugar) to pair with your Pavlova. Simply delicious!!

RECIPE 12:

Gingerbread Man

FRENCH NAME: *Homme de pain d'épices*

BACKGROUND INFO

A gingerbread man is a cookie or biscuit made from gingerbread, usually in the shape of a stylised caricature of a human being, although other shapes, especially seasonal themes (Christmas, Halloween, Easter, etc..) and characters are common too.

The first documented instance of figure-shaped gingerbread biscuits was at the court of Elizabeth I of England.

COOKING NOTES

Preparing gingerbread man can teach you many key skills such as how to make **gingerbread dough**, how to use a **cookie cutter**, how to use a **rolling pin** and how to use candy for decoration.

INGREDIENTS

Gingerbread man

-	Butter	100g
-	Sugar	100g
-	Honey	100g
-	Egg yolk	1
-	Flour	250g
-	Salt	½ teaspoon
-	Baking powder	½ teaspoon
-	Baking soda	½ teaspoon

Royal icing

-	Icing sugar	200g
-	Egg white	1
-	Lemon Juice	½ lemon

METHOD

- Beat softened butter & sugar, together in a large bowl until creamy.
- Add honey & egg yolk beat for about 2 minutes.
- Whisk flour, 1/2 teaspoon salt, and baking soda together in a bowl.
- Gradually stir flour mixture into butter mixture until dough is combined.
- Place the dough in a fridge for 30 minutes minimum.
- Roll the dough out to a 0.5cm (¼ inch) thickness on a lightly floured surface. Using cookie cutters, cut out the gingerbread men shapes and place on the baking tray, leaving a gap between them.
- Cook for 7 minutes at 200 °C or until lightly golden-brown.
- Leave on the tray for 10 minutes and then move to a wire rack to finish cooling.
- When cooled, decorate with the writing icing and decorations.

REFLECTION

With this recipe I learned:

____

____

____

When I make this again, one thing I might do differently is:

____

____

____

The end product tasted really:

____

____

____

CHEF JEAN'S TOP TIPS

THE END

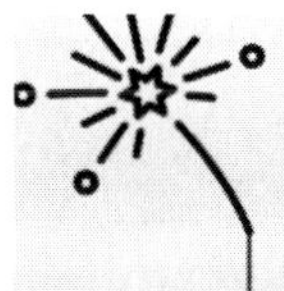
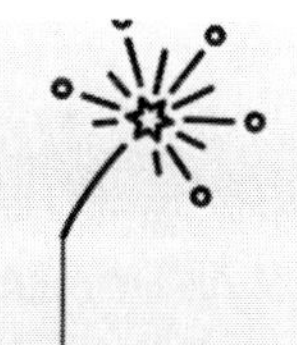

Congratulations!

You have made it to the end of Volume 1!

You now know 12 of the most popular French recipes and are becoming quite the young chef!

You have learnt some really important cooking techniques that can be transferred to other recipes!

If you'd like to know more, join me again for Volume 2! With more exciting recipes and more great cooking tips and tricks!

À bientôt les amis!

Made in United States
Cleveland, OH
11 July 2026